Is this Bangers?
Or is this Mash?
It's Bangers with a spoon.

D0994734

He has a tin
and a jam pot with him.

2

He digs up six
fat, wiggly worms.

Then he puts them
in the tin.

4

He puts some mud
in the tin with them.

Then he takes the tin
to the house.

He puts it on the table.
Then he runs off.

Mash comes in
with a spoon.

What's in that tin?

He puts his nose
in the tin.

Then he gets out
the six wiggly worms
with the spoon.

He puts them
in Mum's tea-pot.

12

Mum comes in
to get the tea.

Then Dad comes in
for his tea.

Dad sits at the table.

"What's this then?
Worms for tea!"